Labor Day

Mir Tamim Ansary

Heinemann Library
Des Plaines, Illinois

Printed in Hong Kong / China

03 02 01 00 99
10 9 8 7 6 5 4 3 2 1

Library of Congress Cataloging-in-Publication Data
Ansary, Mir Tamim, 1954-
    Labor Day / Mir Tamim Ansary.
        p.   cm. — (Holiday histories)
    Includes bibliographical references and index.
    Summary: Introduces Labor Day, explaining the historical events
behind it, how it became a holiday, and how it is observed.
    ISBN 1-57572-703-X (lib. bdg.)
    1. Labor Day—Juvenile literature. [1. Labor Day. 2. Holidays.]
I. Title. II. Series: Ansary, Mir Tamim. Holiday histories.
HD7791.A57 1998
394.264—dc21   98-13720
                                                          CIP
                                                          AC

Acknowledgments
The publisher would like to thank the following for permission to reproduce
photographs:

Cover: UPI/Corbis-Bettmann

Photo Edit/Ulrike Welsch, p. 5; Photo Edit/David Young-Wolff, p. 6; Super Stock, pp. 7,
22; The Granger Collection, pp. 8, 10, 11, 12, 14, 17, 20, 25; Corbis-Bettmann, pp. 9,
13, 16, 24; Photo Researchers, Inc., p. 15; UPI/Corbis-Bettmann, pp. 18, 19; AP/Wide
World, pp. 21, 27; Photo Edit/Bill Aron, p. 23; Photo Edit/Mark Richards, p. 26;
Gamma-Liason/Gilles Mingasson, p. 28; Photo Edit/Michael Newman p. 29.

Every effort has been made to contact copyright holders of any material reproduced
in this book. Any omissions will be rectified in subsequent printings if notice is given to
the publisher.

Some words are shown in bold, **like this**. You can find
out what they mean by looking in the glossary.

Contents

The Last Summer Holiday

Today is Monday. Why is the park so crowded? Because this is Labor Day. Schools are closed, and most grown-ups do not have to work.

Can you smell the hot dogs? Many families have cookouts on this day. Some families go camping. This is the last three-day weekend of the summer.

4

Why Do We Rest?

Tomorrow we put away our swim suits and sandals. Fall is coming. But today we will have fun outdoors. That is what people do on Labor Day.

That is what people did when your grandparents were young. But labor means "work." Why don't people work on Labor Day? You'll find the answer in history.

Work in the Past

Long ago, most people worked on farms. They grew crops. They raised animals. The work was hard and slow.

Everything people needed was made by hand.
Such **goods** cost a lot of money. So most
people made their own goods if they could.

The Machine Age

ROLLING A RAIL

SAWING A RAIL

Then, around two hundred years ago, a big change started. Special kinds of machines were **invented**. These machines could do the same jobs as people, only faster.

10

Rich people bought the machines and set up factories. They used machines to make cheap **goods**. One factory could make enough cloth for thousands of people.

A Changing World

Machines took over many farm jobs, too. Each machine could do the work of many people. So machines put a lot of people out of work.

Many people moved from farms to cities. They went to work in factories, running machines. Hundreds of people worked side by side in big factories.

The First Factories

The first factories were dirty and noisy and dangerous. Workers were paid very little money. Many had to work twelve hours a day, seven days a week.

In many poor families, children had to work. They didn't go to school. They even had to work on weekends.

Labor Unions Are Born

Workers who complained could be **fired**. Factory owners didn't have to worry about losing them. They could easily find other workers.

At last, some workers formed groups called
labor unions. Union workers stood up for
each other. If one worker was fired, other
workers might **refuse** to work.

Going on Strike

Refusing to work was called going on strike.
A union strike could shut down a factory.
Labor unions began using this power to
ask for changes.

Factory owners tried to get new workers.
But the unions blocked the factory gates
to keep new workers out. Sometimes fights
began.

Unions Grow

The police had to break up the fights. Often they sided with the owners. They beat up **strikers.** They put union workers in jail.

Labor unions kept growing. New ones kept forming. Unions joined together to form bigger groups. Samuel Gompers led a group with millions of members.

Better Days
for Workers

Slowly, **unions** began to make a difference. Workers were paid more money and they didn't have to work as long. They didn't have to work weekends anymore. Laws were passed to make work places safer.

One new law said that factories could not use children as workers. That's why American children never work in factories anymore. They go to school instead.

The First Labor Day

In 1882, a union leader named Peter Maguire came up with an idea. He said America should have a holiday to **honor** its workers.

Congress agreed. In 1892, the first Monday in September was made a holiday. That was the first Labor Day.

25

Workers Today

Today, fewer Americans work in factories. More and more people work in places like offices and restaurants. Many people work at home. But they are still workers.

And in many cities, Labor Day is still a day
to **honor** workers. Look at this huge Labor
Day parade in Detroit, Michigan.

Workers in Your Life

You may not be a worker yet. But workers play a big part in your life. They made your toys, your clothes, your house.

Workers made almost everything you use
or need. All Americans have a reason to
celebrate Labor Day.

Important Dates

Labor Day

1733	The first cloth-making machines are invented
1785	Steam engines are first used to drive machines
1833	The first **labor unions** form in the United States
1869	Knights of Labor, a union of unions, is founded
1882	Peter Maguire wants a holiday to **honor** labor
1886	American Federation of Labor is founded
1892	Congress declares Labor Day a holiday
1894	Federal troops break up the Pullman Strike
1901	Membership in the A.F.L. tops one million
1917	Railroad workers win the eight-hour day
1935	National Labor Relations Act laws are passed to protect union workers in the U.S.

Glossary

Congress group of elected people that makes the laws of the United States

fired forced to leave a job

goods things people use

honor to show respect for something or someone

invented thought of and made for the first time

labor union group of workers that tries to make their jobs better

refuse to not do something when asked

strikers workers who are on strike

More Books to Read

Cedano, Maria. *Cesar Chavez: Labor Leader.* Brookfield, Conn: Millbrook Press, 1993.

Penner, Lucille. *Celebration: The Story of American Holidays.* New York: Simon & Schuster Childrens, 1993.

Scott, Geoffrey. *Labor Day.* Minneapolis, Minn: Lerner Publishing Group, 1982.

Index